THE
COMPLETE BOOK
OF THE SEASONS

Sally Tagholm

NEW YORK

Managing Editor   Melissa Fairley
Editor   Hannah Wilson
Coordinating Editor   Sarah Snavely
Designer   Jane Buckley
Production Controller   Debbie Otter
DTP Manager   Nicky Studdart
Picture Research Manager   Jane Lambert
Picture Research Assistant   Rachael Swann
Artwork Archivists   Wendy Allison and Steve Robinson

The publisher would like to thank the following illustrators:
Susanna Addario, Mike Atkinson, Andrea Brun, John Butler,
Peter Dennis (Linda Rogers Associates), Ray Grinaway, Ian Jackson (Wildlife Art),
Kevin Madison, Sebastian Quidley, Mike Saunders, Roger Stewart (Kevin Jones Associates),
Richard Ward, Gareth Williams, and Dan Wright

The publisher would also like to thank the following for supplying photographs:
Corbis: 12tl, 24bl; Ardea London: 26tl; NHPA: 26cl; Corbis: 30bl; Science Photo Library,
Tom McHugh: 45br; Frank Lane Picture Agency, David Hosking: 46c;
www.osf.uk.com, Scott Winer: 49bl; Popperfoto, David Joiner: 50tl;
Eye Ubiquitous, ©John Dakers: 52bl; Still Pictures, Julio Etchart: 66bl;
Still Pictures, Ron Giling: 84bl; Popperfoto: 90bl; P. A. Photos: 93cr
Every effort has been made to trace the copyright holders of the photographs.
The publisher apologizes for any inconvenience caused.

KINGFISHER
a Houghton Mifflin Company imprint
215 Park Avenue South
New York, New York 10003
www.houghtonmifflinbooks.com

First published in 2002
2 4 6 8 10 9 7 5 3 1

1TR/0502/TWP/CLSN(CLSN)/150ENSOMA

LIBRARY OF CONGRESS CATALOGING-IN-PUBLICATION DATA
has been applied for.

ISBN 0-7534-5457-2

Printed in Singapore

CONTENTS

THE SEASONS 4

CHANGING SEASONS 6
The four seasons 8
Hot and cold 10
Wet and dry 12
Wind and waves 14

SPRING 16
Spring showers 18
Spring flowers 20
Pond life 22
Spring farming 24
Spring cleaning 26
In the park 28
Spring nights 30
St. Patrick's Day 32
Bun Bang Fai 34

SUMMER 36
Summer Sun 38
Keeping cool 40
Summer insects 42
Summertime 44
Summer farming 46
Summer vacations 48
Summer sports 50

Midnight sun festival 52
Verona opera festival 54

FALL 56
Fall winds 58
Fall colors 60
Fall fauna 62
Fall farming 64
Fall and us 66
Up in the air 68
Thanksgiving 70
Chinese moon festival 72

WINTER 74
Winter chills 76
Hibernation 78
Migration 80
Wintertime 82
Winter farming 84
Winter playtime 86
Winter sports 88
Sapporo's snow festival 90
New Year's 92

SEASONAL EVENTS 94

INDEX 96

THE SEASONS

As the year goes by, neatly divided into months and weeks and days, the seasons unfold and change, transforming the world around us and the things we do. Spring, summer, fall, and winter sometimes creep up slowly, one sliding seamlessly into the next, but at other times they arrive unannounced, a sudden dramatic change, impossible to miss.

CHANGING SEASONS

In most countries there are four seasons every year — spring, summer, fall, and winter. Each one lasts for about three months and has certain weather and temperatures connected with it. The hours of daylight also vary enormously according to the season. On a cold, dark winter's evening it is hard to remember the long, hot days of summer — let alone splashing in the sea or lying in the sun.

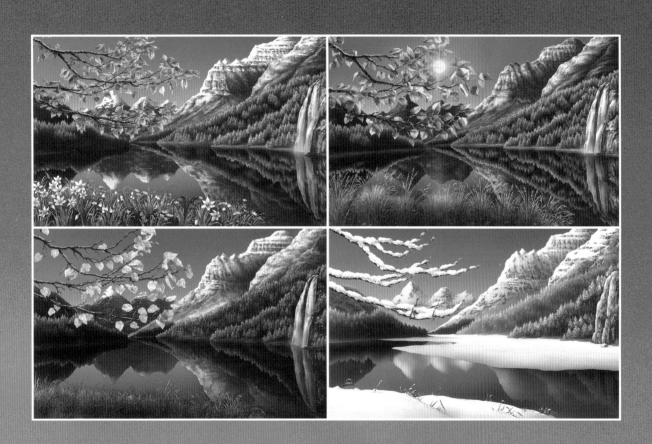

The four seasons

From the beginning of time people have recognized the importance of the seasons and celebrated them in many different ways. No matter where you live, what language you speak, or which calendar you follow, the seasons follow their own rhythm in a never-ending cycle. It is the same pattern year after year. Each season is different from the next and is just as important, changing the natural world around us in its own unique way.

Spring announces birth and renewal, while the summer brings sun and warmth to make everything ripen and grow. In the fall, nature begins to slow down as it gets ready for its long winter sleep. People also change with the seasons— our energy levels wax and wane with the sun. In the short, dark days of winter we curl up and keep warm at home, just like the seeds under the bleak, bare ground. As soon as spring arrives we open doors and windows and want to be outside, enjoying the fresh air. In the summer we soak up the sun like sunflowers in the fields, and in the fall we get out our gloves and scarves, knowing that winter will soon be here.

Other planets in the solar system also have seasons. These are caused by the way the planets tilt or by their varying distance from the Sun as they orbit it in huge, uneven loops. Mars has four seasons, just like Earth, but because a Martian year is as long as two years on Earth, its seasons are also much longer. Mercury, on the other hand, has no atmosphere, so there is no wind or rain and no protection against the Sun's heat. With days and nights each lasting about three Earth months and with the planet swinging closer and farther from the Sun, temperatures can range from 788°F to –292°F (420°C to –180°C). The planet Uranus has very unusual seasons. The South Pole has a summer lasting 42 years, when the Sun never sets, and the opposite Pole is dark for 42 years.

In recent years many of the world's leading scientists have issued warnings that Earth is warming up because of pollution from burning fossil fuels. It is believed that global warming is causing weather patterns to change as the ice caps melt and the sea levels rise. It is also possible that it is making the seasons shift slightly, with earlier springs, longer summers, and milder winters.

Every year the seasons change because of the way Earth spins around on its own axis as it orbits the Sun. It rotates tilted to one side at an angle of 23.5°. This means that first one half of the globe and then the other leans toward the Sun. In December, when the North Pole tilts away from the Sun, countries in the Northern Hemisphere have winter. At the same time the South Pole is tilted toward the Sun, so countries in the Southern Hemisphere are having their summer. In June the opposite happens to both hemispheres as Earth's tilt changes.

Hot and cold

In some countries near the equator it is hot all year round, and the sun is always high overhead. In the polar regions the temperature rarely rises above the freezing point.

In Antarctica the sun completely disappears during the winter, and temperatures can drop to –58°F (–50°C). The size of the continent almost doubles as the pack ice surrounding it freezes.

Most deserts are hot all year round, and it hardly ever rains. There are no clouds to block the sun, and temperatures reach extremes. Lack of water is a problem for both plants and animals, but they have evolved and adapted to cope with the conditions. The Bactrian, or Asian, camel can survive for long periods (5 to 7 days) without food or water because it stores fats and oils, which give it energy, in its two humps.

The adult male penguins huddle together to conserve heat, taking turns to stand on the outside where freezing winds sweep past.

But the flightless birds that live there are well adapted to the bitter cold, insulated with layers of fat, thick skin, and dense feathers that trap warm air. Emperor penguins live in colonies near the sea and breed during the harsh winters. The female lays a single egg and disappears to find food, leaving the male to incubate the egg by himself. For nine weeks he balances the egg on his feet, where it is protected by his soft, warm body. By the time the female returns, the male will have lost up to one third of his body weight. She now feeds the newly hatched chick, and her partner sets off for the sea.

11

Wet and dry

Some regions a few degrees north and south of the equator, such as parts of South America and Africa, are hot and dry for most of the year. They have one or sometimes two rainy seasons every year.

In South Asia the summer monsoon season lasts from June to September each year. The torrential rains blow in from the ocean as the direction of the wind changes, coming from the southwest. The southern tip of India is the first to receive the long-awaited rains—its arrival is vital for next year's crops. But if the rains are even heavier than usual, they can cause terrible flooding. In 1988, 28 million people lost their homes in Bangladesh.

The grasslands—or savannas—of Africa, South America, and northern Australia all suffer during the long, hot, dry season. During this time the landscape is parched by the sun—the grass dries up and turns yellow, and the trees lose their leaves. Trees such as the acacia and baobab survive because they have very long roots that tap groundwater from deep beneath the surface. The baobab also has a huge fireproof trunk that stores water like a sponge. The bushmen of the Kalahari Desert use hollow grass for straws to drink the precious water inside the trunks.

In order to
survive, herds
of grazing
animals such as
zebras and elephants
have to travel huge
distances over the plains
in search of water. Smaller
creatures such as meerkats and
ground squirrels burrow under
the ground to escape the heat and
avoid losing too much moisture.

Wind and Waves

Late spring and early in the summer is the tornado—or "twister"—season in the Great Plains region. Tornadoes also occur in Australia, Canada, the United Kingdom, Italy, Japan, and central Asia.

Tornadoes can form suddenly when warm, moist air cools and rises to form great towering thunderclouds. Cold air rushes in to replace the rising air, creating strong winds. If the winds rotate faster and faster, a funnel-shaped tornado is formed, stretching down from the thundercloud.

Tornadoes get their name from the Latin word for twist or turn. When they first form, they are made up of millions of tiny water droplets—just like any cloud. But as soon as they touch the ground they start to suck up soil and dirt and turn almost black. They can pick up anything in their path— houses, cars, buses, and animals—and the wind speeds inside the tornado can reach up to 500 mph (800km/h).

Tropical revolving storms called hurricanes occur over the Atlantic from June 1 to November 30. They form over the ocean when warm air rises so fast that it creates a region of intense low pressure beneath it. More and more air is pulled in, creating a huge, spiraling weather system. When the wind speed reaches 75 mph (120km/h), it officially becomes a hurricane.

Hurricanes can be 250 mi. (400km) wide with winds spiraling furiously inside. To the north of the equator they blow in a counterclockwise direction—to the south of the equator they blow in a clockwise direction. At the very center, or "eye," of the storm everything is still and calm, and the temperatures are very high. Similar storms are known as typhoons when they are over the Pacific Ocean and cyclones over the Indian Ocean.

A huge storm often accompanies a hurricane, cyclone, or typhoon as it races across the ocean toward the land. The waters are sucked up by the low pressure, forming a gigantic wall of water. Some waves reach a height of 100 ft. (30m) and cause severe flooding in low-lying coastal areas such as Bangladesh, Pakistan, and northwest India. In February of 1953 a massive storm surge flooded areas of The Netherlands, killing 2,000 people. In 1969 Hurricane Camille (hurricanes are usually given names, alternating between male and female) devastated the coasts of Florida and Mississippi, and a 27-ft. (8.2-m) storm surge drowned 300 people. Meteorologists are constantly working out better ways of predicting hurricanes to try and save lives.

SPRING

Spring brings new life to the world after the quiet, cold winter months. The weather begins to get warmer, and the days last longer. Bright flowers appear, creatures emerge from hibernation, and birds start singing in the early morning. Farmers are busy in their fields, planting new crops and tending the newborn lambs.

Spring showers

As spring arrives the days get longer, and the ground begins to warm up after the long winter months. But the weather can change very quickly, with bright sunshine one moment and rain the next.

Spring is famous for its sudden showers and downpours that water the land and encourage everything to grow. It is also the time of year when the sun starts to get stronger and climbs a little higher up in the sky. Brand-new buds begin to appear on the trees, and the first spring flowers come out.

Different kinds of clouds bring changes to the weather. The huge white clouds that are known as cumulonimbus (left) get their name from the Latin words for "puffy" and "rain bearing." They often tower high up in the sky in great thunderstorm formations that look like giant anvils. Like all clouds, they are formed when the water vapor rises and then cools and condenses into millions of tiny droplets of water. These clouds get larger and larger as they collect more and more moisture and then fall to the ground as rain.

Because of the changeable weather, spring is one of the best times of the year for rainbows. They appear suddenly when the sun comes out from behind a cloud but it is still raining. The colors of the rainbow always come in the same order—with red at the top, followed by orange, yellow, green, blue, indigo, and violet.

Spring is a good time to put on your raincoat and boots and splash around in puddles. The first waterproof boot was invented in 1815 and was named after England's Duke of Wellington.

A raindrop acts like a prism, bending and refracting the rays of the sun to form a rainbow. It breaks the sunlight up into the seven colors of the rainbow, which is called the spectrum.

A thermometer measures how hot or cold the air is. Thermometers contain some mercury or alcohol, which moves up a narrow tube when it gets hot and falls back down when it is cold.

19

Spring flowers

In early spring the tiny pink flowers of the spring beauty creep across woods and line creeks like a starry carpet. They open only when the sun is shining. Spring beauty is sometimes known as "fairy spuds" because it grows from a small bulb that looks like a little potato.

Dangling catkins (male), or lambs' tails, open very early in the spring before leaves appear on the hazel tree. They have been developing since the fall, and each one has more than 100 tiny flowers on it. The catkins release their yellow pollen as they swing in the wind.

After the bleak, bare days of winter tender new shoots push through the ground as spring arrives. Tight buds uncurl and open as if by magic, turning into bright spring flowers and opening their faces to the sun.

Many flowers that bloom in the spring—such as crocuses, daffodils, hyacinths, and tulips—grow from round bulbs or knobbly corms. They are planted in the fall and spend the winter buried safely underground, waiting for the first hint of warm weather before they start sprouting.

All kinds of bulbs are cultivated in different countries around the world, but Holland is especially famous for its bulb farms. In the spring huge fields of flowers stretch as far as the eye can see, like splashes of color in a giant paint palette. But long ago, in the 1600s, some bulbs were so rare and valuable that single specimens were sold for incredible sums of money. One tulip bulb, known as a "Semper Augustus," was sold for 3,000 Dutch guilders—the equivalent of $1,600.

Daffodils are probably the most popular spring flowers, with their long, green stems and friendly, nodding faces. Strangely enough, the bulb and leaves contain poisonous crystals, which means that they are eaten by only a handful of insects.

Pond life

For most of the year a pond is a peaceful place with only a few ducks or moorhens to be seen. In the spring, however, it becomes a hive of activity as creatures both above and below the surface of the water prepare for the breeding season.

Dragonfly nymphs change their skin as they grow, and after the fifth or sixth change their wings begin to form. They climb out of the water, clinging tightly to the weeds, and shed their skins for the last time, emerging as beautiful dragonflies.

Pond plants, such as water irises, often grow along the water's edge. Water irises, sometimes called yellow flags, bring a vivid splash of color to ponds in the spring. Water lilies, on the other hand, anchor their long roots in mud at the pond's bottom, while their broad leaves float on the water's surface.

The great diving beetle eats tadpoles, pond snails, and small fish. In the spring the female lays her eggs inside the stems of water plants. When the larva hatches, it looks like a strange, pale, shrimplike insect. It clings to plants and weeds so that it does not float to the surface.

In the breeding season the male smooth newt is brightly colored and has a wavy crest along his back. He often performs a special courtship dance, arching his back and flicking his tail to impress the female. She lays her eggs one at a time in a nice, safe place— under a leaf or a waterweed.

In the spring male woodpeckers mark out their territory and attract females by drumming sharply on the bark of a tree with their beaks. It is kind of like a secret code—each bird pecking out his message to a slightly different rhythm, letting everybody know that he is there. The males usually stop doing this when they begin nesting.

Moorhens usually build their nests out of old, dried-up water plants and reeds near the water's edge. Sometimes they use old nests abandoned by other birds in bushes nearby. The female lays a clutch of between 5 and 11 eggs, which is incubated by both parents.

Soon after baby ducks hatch out of their eggs, they follow their mother to the pond, splashing happily into the water. They can swim immediately, and before long they learn to find food for themselves. When these young mallards are fully grown, the males will be more colorful than the females.

Every spring during the breeding season, frogs come back to the pond to mate. The females lay their eggs in clumps of clear jelly that float just below the surface of the water. These are known as frog spawn. The tiny tadpoles that hatch from the eggs gradually grow legs, turning into small froglets after about 12 or 13 weeks.

23

Spring farming

The farming year has followed the cycle of the seasons since people first started cultivating the land. Each year follows the same familiar pattern, which shapes farmers' lives all over the world.

Spring is one of the busiest times of the year, with many different jobs to be done on the farm. As soon as the last chills of winter disappear, the fields are prepared and planted with seeds for summer crops, and cattle are led out from their barns to new pastures.

Lambing, which usually starts in late winter, goes on throughout the early spring. The grass is lush and green after all the rain, and the ewes (female sheep) produce rich and nourishing milk that helps their wobbling lambs grow. Soon the lambs are strong enough to race around the field and play in the spring sunshine. They are weaned from their mothers by the time they are six months old.

Rice is the staple food of over half of the people in the world, and it needs a warm climate and plenty of water to grow. At first the crop is planted in dry fields, but as soon as it starts to sprout, the seedlings are transplanted by hand to rice paddies. These are pools of water that have been dug out and prepared with a small wall of soil around each one. Sometimes, to make sure that the bottom of the paddy is soft enough for the roots of seedlings, the farmer drives his cattle around in circles to break up the soil. The seedlings are carefully planted out one at a time under the water in neat, straight lines. Later on in the year, when the rice is ripe, the paddies are drained before the harvest.

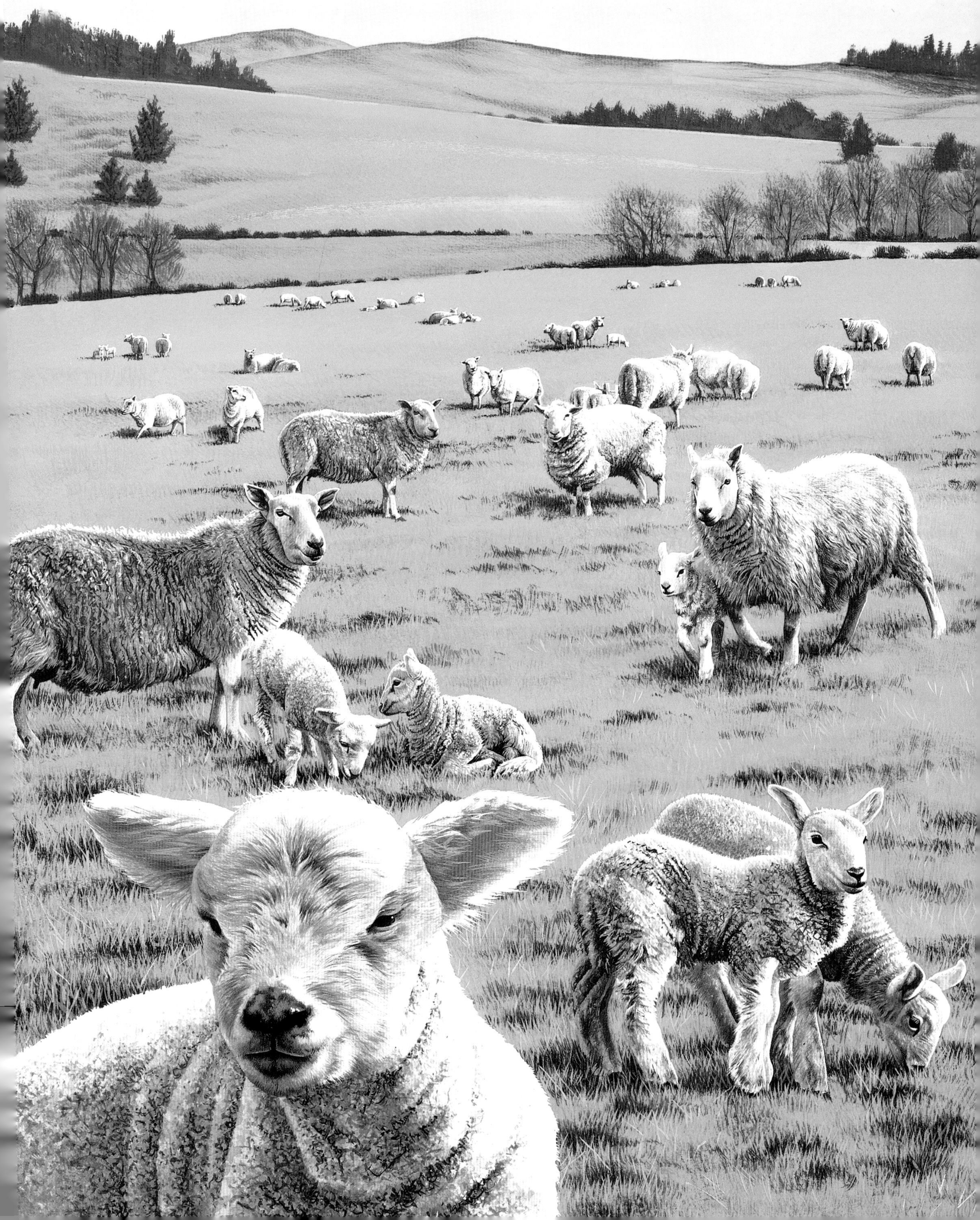

Spring cleaning

Spring is traditionally the season of rebirth and renewal, when the whole world seems to wake up after the long, cold months of winter. Everything is filled with new energy—including us!

Boatyards, marinas, and harbors hum with activity in the spring, and the smell of paint fills the air. It is the time of year when boats are repainted and repaired to get them ready for the water.

The bright spring sunshine that floods in through the windows shows all the dust and dirt of winter. So it is not surprising that many people give their home a good cleaning.

Nowadays we have all kinds of machines and gadgets that help us clean the house. Soon we might even have robots to sweep the floor or polish the table for us. But long ago, when everything had to be done by hand, spring-cleaning the house could take days or even weeks. Open fires that smoked and blazed all winter long, producing plenty of ash and soot, used to make everything very dirty.

The first successful vacuum cleaner, invented in 1901, was the size of a rowboat and was operated by four to six people. The first stand-up vacuum cleaner (to be used by one person) was developed in 1907.

Traditionally spring-cleaning used to start around the time of the vernal—or spring—equinox, when days and nights are the same length. This is also the first day of spring—March 20 or 21 in the Northern Hemisphere and September 22 or 23 in the Southern Hemisphere. From this point the days will be getting much longer and warmer, so you can put away your winter clothes and begin thinking about the summer. It is also time to tidy up—perhaps even to find lost treasures that disappeared many months ago.

Eastre was the ancient goddess of spring in northern Europe and was often pictured with a basket of eggs and a hare or rabbit. She represented the rebirth of earth and of all growing things.

27

In the park

As the spring arrives and the days get longer
bright sunshine casts its spell over the world again.
It lures people out into the fresh, mild air—heavy winter
clothes can be put away and forgotten for another year.

The park, which has been still and bare for most of the
winter, is beginning to stir. Some of the trees are dotted
with tiny green buds, and early pink blossoms have suddenly
appeared. The birds are building their nests and getting ready
to lay their eggs, and ducks are hungry, waiting to be fed.

On bright spring days there are many people in the park,
enjoying the sunshine. The smell of freshly cut grass fills the
air for the first time since last summer. The groundskeepers
have been busy getting everything ready for another year—
painting and planting. Dogs bark and race around, chasing
their tails and fetching sticks and balls. Children play on
the swings, swoop down the slides, and ride their bicycles.

There are special skate parks where skateboarders can enjoy themselves. There is usually a large concrete half pipe in the middle of the park, which looks like a gigantic letter "U." Skaters practice their most daring tricks on it, speeding up and down the smooth curves at high speeds and flying through the air. They always wear helmets on their heads, pads to protect their knees and elbows, and baggy clothes so they can move around comfortably and safely. There are many different tricks, but one of the most popular is an "air," when all four wheels of the skateboard are lifted off the ground at the same time.

Some trees
grow leaves
and are covered
with a layer of green,
while the branches
of others are still bare.
The silver birch and the
willow are two of the first
to show their new spring leaves.

In some parks dogs
have to be kept on
a leash. In city parks
there is usually a dog
run, a fenced-in area
where dogs are free
to run and play.

Spring nights

Warm spring nights are perfect for stargazing—especially if you have a pair of binoculars or a telescope. You can explore the universe from your own backyard.

Each spring new constellations—or patterns of stars—appear in the night sky, marking the passing of the seasons. In the Northern Hemisphere, Orion and its neighboring constellations slowly drift out of sight, and others come into view.

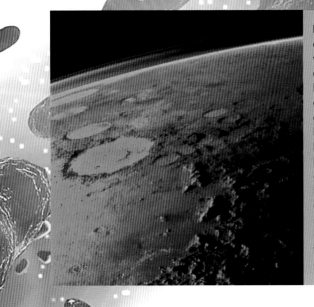

Mars—known as the Red Planet—rotates on its axis with a tilt of 23.98°, which is very similar to Earth's, and its four seasons are opposite in the Northern and Southern hemispheres, just like ours. But each season on Mars is about twice as long as one of ours because a Martian year is twice as long as an Earth year. Spring on Mars brings warmer weather after the long, harsh winter, when daytime temperatures can drop to –76°F (–60°C), and nights can be as cold as –148°F (–100°C). As spring arrives so do raging winds and huge dust storms, which make the atmosphere hazy and heavy. The polar ice cap—made of frozen carbon dioxide—starts to evaporate and becomes much smaller by the summer.

Spring in the Northern Hemisphere is a good time to observe meteor showers such as the Lyrids in April and the Eta Aquarids in May.

Leo, the lion, is one of the most spectacular constellations of all. The head and front paws look like a backward question mark made out of stars. This is often known as the Sickle. At the bottom of it there is a brilliant star called Regulus, which means "little king." It is approximately 85 light-years away from Earth and shines 160 times brighter than our Sun—it also has a bluish-white tinge.

On clear, moonless nights you might see some meteors streaking across the sky. Meteor showers are caused when Earth passes through a cloud of space debris left by a passing comet.

St. Patrick's Day

The feast of St. Patrick, the patron saint of Ireland, is a national holiday on March 17. It is celebrated by people all around the world—whether or not they are Irish. In the United States millions of Americans hold huge street parades across the country.

St. Patrick lived more than 1,500 years ago and is generally believed to have brought Christianity to Ireland. He was in fact born in Wales in A.D. 385, but he spent 30 years of his life traveling around Ireland setting up churches, monasteries, and schools. It is said that he gave a sermon from a hilltop that drove all the snakes out of Ireland. Some people think this was another way of saying he converted the pagans to Christianity.

There is a carnival feeling in the air on St. Patrick's Day—and everyone enjoys the decorated floats, marching bands, and traditional Irish dancers. Some people join the parade dressed in green, their faces and hair also painted green. Or they put on costumes to dress up—often as leprechauns, the little shoemakers from Irish folktales. Everyone wears a shamrock, the three-leafed clover associated with St. Patrick.

The first public St. Patrick's Day celebrations in the United States were held in Boston in 1737. The first St. Patrick's Day Parade took place when Irish soldiers serving in the English Army marched through New York City in 1762.

The beginning of spring is celebrated by the Hindu festival of Holi in India. It can last for two or three days. On the night of the full moon during the spring harvest a large bonfire is lit, and the direction of the flames is believed to show which land will be especially fertile in the coming year. Garlands of cow dung (cows are sacred in India) are thrown in the fire. Offerings of wheat and grains are made, and coconuts—symbols of new life—are roasted in the fire. It is also a festival of color, symbolizing fertility. People cover each other in colored paints (gulal).

33

Bun Bang Fai

Each year, in the second week of May, a rocket festival known as Bun Bang Fai is held in northeastern Thailand. It is the end of the long dry season and traditionally the time of year when farmers pray for rain for their crops.

According to legend there was once a rain god named Vassakan, who loved being worshiped with fire. A rocket—or Bang Fai—was made by local people and sent high up in the sky to where the rain god lived. The people hoped that Vassakan would respond and bless them with rain.

The two-day festival has been celebrated for centuries, and today people come from all over the world to watch the dazzling displays. On the first day of the festival there are parades, and on the second day the rockets are launched.

It is believed that if the rockets shoot high up in the air, the village will be blessed with rain and there will be plenty of food in the coming season. Before the launching ceremony Buddhist monks bless the rockets.

Toonik Tyme celebrates the coming of spring in Nunavut, a Canadian territory in the eastern Arctic. The traditional Inuit festivities include igloo-building competitions and a special appearance by the "Tuniq," who is a little bit like an Arctic Easter bunny but dresses up in caribou skins. Inuit games are played, and there are snowmobile and dog-team races. Inuit dogs, known as *Qimmiq* in Inuktitut, are perfectly adapted to the Arctic climate and live on a diet of meat and fat. These dogs have lived in the Arctic for over 4,000 years.

The rockets are all homemade and are constructed from bamboo, or wooden tubes, with colorful designs painted on them. Competitions are held for the biggest rocket or for the one that can fly the highest. Some of the rockets are huge—up to 30 ft. (9m) long—and packed with up to 55 lbs (25kg) of gunpowder.

SUMMER

The sun is high overhead and at its strongest during the long, hot days of summer. Flowers and fields are in full bloom, and bees are busy collecting pollen and nectar. Crops ripen slowly in the warmth, and summer fruits are ready to pick. The beach is crowded with vacationers enjoying the sunshine.

Summer Sun

The Sun is our nearest star and the source of all light, warmth, and life on Earth. Its yearly journey marks the passing of the seasons. In the summer it travels much higher each day and its rays are stronger, encouraging everything to grow.

The Sun has been burning for around five billion years. The temperature at its core is 59 million°F (15 million°C), and its light travels at about 186,420 mi. (300,000km) per second. This means that it takes approximately eight-and-a-half minutes for sunlight to reach us.

Because Earth rotates at an angle and is tilted to one side, the Sun appears directly overhead at different latitudes during the year. In the Northern Hemisphere the summer solstice (June 20 or 21) is the time when the Sun reaches its most northerly point, over the Tropic of Cancer (23°, 27 minutes North). The longest day of the year, with the most hours of sunlight, falls within this time—generally known as the beginning of summer. It has always been an important time of year, celebrated by different religions and cultures around the world. The word "solstice" comes from the Latin word *solstitium*, which means "sun standing still." This is just what the sun appears to do—changing its angle extremely slowly from day to day.

Activity on the surface of the Sun, such as sunspots, flares, and solar storms, follows an 11-year cycle. At its peak the wind can rise to gale force, and the ensuing effects can be felt all over Earth.

The Campbell Stokes Sunshine Recorder counts the daily hours of sunshine. A glass ball focuses the sun's rays onto a piece of cardboard, burning a horizontal line (or dots if the Sun moves in or out of the clouds).

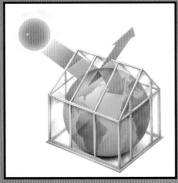

Many leading scientists now believe that Earth is warming up because of the greenhouse effect. This means that some gases, such as carbon dioxide, trap energy from the sunlight and do not allow heat to escape back into space.

It is not the hottest point of the summer—it usually takes
another few weeks for Earth to warm up. In the Southern
Hemisphere the opposite is happening at the same time,
and it is the winter solstice and the shortest day.

Although the summer is usually the hottest time of the year,
Earth is in fact farthest away from the Sun at this
time of year. This is because it does not
travel around the Sun in an exact circle
but in an oval loop. In January we
are 93 million mi. (150 million km)
away from the Sun, whereas
in July we are 96 million mi.
(155 million km) from it.

WARNING: You should never look at
the Sun directly and certainly never
through a telescope or binoculars—
you could be permanently blinded.

Keeping cool

Many creatures have evolved so that they can cool down automatically when the weather gets very hot. Others have to change their behavior to stay out of the sun and avoid the boiling heat.

The crocodile, a cold-blooded creature, soaks up warmth from the sun and then lies with its mouth wide open. The skin inside its mouth is very thin with many blood vessels near the surface. As air circulates, moisture evaporates from its mouth.

The horse needs shade and plenty of water to drink when temperatures are high. It sweats all over its body to try and keep itself cool. The sweat contains a protein that forms a lather—like whipped egg whites—when the horse is extremely hot.

Most mammals have special sweat glands that start working when it gets hot. The glands cover the skin with moisture, which then evaporates and cools the body down.

Some mammals, like rodents and opossums, have a completely different technique. They produce saliva in their mouths and then lick it all over their fur. Many other animals cool down by splashing around in a pond or a river.

The camel can survive extreme heat and last for almost one week without water. The long hair on its head, throat, neck, and hump helps protect it from sunburn. Another mammal that is physically adapted to extreme heat is the tiny fennec fox. Its enormous ears act as conductors to help get rid of the heat. Some snakes and lizards keep cool by opening their mouths as wide as they can. The desert iguana even pants like a dog with its tongue hanging out.

The dog does not have any sweat glands—except on the pads of its feet. It lowers its body temperature by opening its mouth and panting to allow moisture to evaporate from its lungs, cooling it down.

To keep cool the elephant sprays water over itself with its trunk, rolls in cool, wet mud, and flaps its ears to lower the temperature of its blood circulating around its body.

41

Summer insects

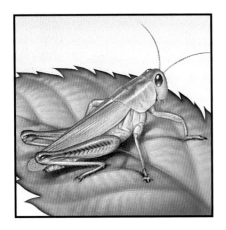

Male grasshoppers and crickets sing in the summer by rubbing together two parts of their body. They do this to attract females. Grasshoppers rub their legs, which have a row of tiny pegs on them, against their front wings. Each kind of grasshopper makes a different sound. Crickets rub an upturned scraper on one front wing along a row of 50–250 teeth on the underside of the other wing.

There are about 1,900 species of fireflies—or lightning bugs—that twinkle and shine on summer nights. They have light organs on the undersides of their bodies, and the males flash special patterns of lights to attract females. The females signal in response—the rhythm and sequence of the light is like a secret code. Some species of fireflies have luminescent larvae called glowworms.

The long, hot days of summer are full of the sounds of insects buzzing, swarming, and scurrying around. They are out and about in their hordes, feeding on newly grown plants. Some eat the leaves, roots, seeds, and sap, while others prefer the nectar and pollen hidden inside flowers.

Honeybees are very busy in the summer when there are plenty of flowers in full bloom, and they sometimes fly as far as 3 mi. (5km) for a good source of nectar. Their favorite flowers are usually blue or purple, followed by yellow or orange. They gather nectar from deep inside the flowers, sucking it up with their long tongues. At the same time they pick up a dusting of pollen on their hind legs. They then fly back to the hive with their precious trophies, which will be used as food for the entire bee colony. The pollen provides protein, and the nectar is converted into honey, which provides carbohydrates.

The colony is a carefully organized community with a queen, up to 500 drones (males), and 60,000 workers (females), all with their individual tasks. When a scout bee has found a good new source of nectar, she communicates this to the other workers by flying in circles and wagging her tail.

Summertime

We all look forward to the summer and being outside, enjoying the sunshine. But the sun can be extremely hot at this time of year and its rays intense. The heat can affect our bodies in different ways.

During the summer it is important to stay out of the sun when it is high up in the sky. In some countries people take a siesta, or nap, during the day when it is hottest.

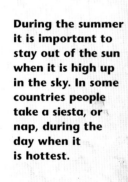

Your body has its own built-in thermostat—the hypothalamus, the brain's "master gland"—which helps the body maintain a constant temperature. During hot weather this gland detects a rise in blood temperature and sends out a signal that causes the blood to flow more rapidly and closer to the surface of the skin, cooling it down. The hypothalamus can also call another natural cooling system into play—sweat. The evaporation of moisture from our skin when we sweat cools our bodies down.

But your body needs extra help in the summer. Drink plenty of fluids regularly to avoid becoming dehydrated, and wear a hat to protect your head. Sun hats come in all shapes and sizes and can be made of cotton, canvas, or even coconut leaves!

Use suntan lotion to protect your skin from the sun's harmful ultraviolet, or UV, rays. It's not just people that need this kind of protection—farmers often rub suntan lotion on their pigs in the summer! Wear white, loose-fitting clothing in the summer. White reflects heat, and loose clothes allow air to circulate, keeping your body cool.

It's not all bad news—the sun is our main source of Vitamin D, which helps the body absorb bone-strengthening calcium and phosphorus. And sunlight stimulates hormones that make us feel happy!

Sundials tell us the time on sunny days. The upright part, the gnomon, casts its shadow onto the hourly markings as earth turns during the day.

In ancient Egypt, where the sun god Re was worshiped, the pharaoh Tutankhamen was kept cool by ostrich-feather fans on long, golden poles.

Before refrigerators and freezers arrived in the 1920s blocks of ice were delivered several times a week and stored in wooden boxes called iceboxes.

Long, sun-filled summer days are perfect for generating electricity from solar panels. Houses and even cars can be powered by the sun.

45

Summer farming

In the summer the sun is at its strongest, and the fields are full of many different crops, such as corn and sunflowers. The farmers make hay from the long, sweet grass when the weather is hot and dry.

Sunflowers are now grown commercially all over the world and are an important crop both for their oil and their seeds. They were originally native to North America, and they were used by native Americans for food and oil.

After they are planted in late spring or early summer sunflowers grow quickly and flower, painting the fields a bright yellow. Their roots go deep and spread out wide, so they are able to find water and survive a certain amount of drought. At first their heads face east in the morning and west in the evening, following the sun on its journey through the sky everyday. Once the flowers have fully opened, they usually face east. This is when the seeds are fully exposed, and the large flower heads act as perfect feeding perches for passing birds.

Strawberries need the right weather conditions to grow, and they can be ruined by a late frost, too much rain, and not enough sun. They can also be spoiled by too much sun and not enough rain. After the flowers bloom on the strawberry plant it takes about one month for the fruit to ripen. In June, when the harvest starts, there are strawberries in all different stages of development on the plants—tiny green berries, big white berries, and ripe red berries. Each plant is picked two or three times a week—unlike other fruits, once the berries have been picked they do not ripen anymore. They are picked, sorted, and packed by hand and then exported worldwide. Some native Americans still celebrate strawberry Thanksgiving in mid- to late-June.

Summer vacations

On a hot summer's day the beach is a perfect playground—as long as you have your swimsuit, a pail and shovel, and a beach ball. And it is a treasure trove, too, where you never know what you will find hidden beneath the sand.

The tide sweeps in and out, constantly cleaning the sand and making it shiny and new. Damp sand is perfect for digging and building sand castles.

As the water washes back it leaves an assortment of interesting things behind, including driftwood shaped by the pounding of the waves, smooth stones, fish skeletons, and seaweed. Usually there are thousands of shells in a dazzling array of shapes and sizes. They are the empty homes of small, soft creatures known as mollusks. There are two kinds of shells: gastropods, which are single often coiled shells, and bivalves, which are paired and joined together by a small hinge.

Seaweed is algae that lives in the sea. There are many different types. Sea belt is known as "poor man's weather glass" because it becomes soft in the rain and brittle in dry weather. When it dries out it becomes covered with a sweet, white substance that gives sea belt its third name—"sugar wrack."

Surfers travel the world with their boards in search of the perfect wave. Many of them head for Hawaii, where the Polynesians invented surfing many centuries ago. They called it wave sliding—*he'e nalu.* The Hawaiian kings used to ride the best boards, which were known as *olos.* They were made of lightweight wili wili wood and could be up to 23 ft. (7m) long. Nowadays, boards are made from foam and fiberglass—usually 6.5 ft. (2m) long for very experienced surfers.

Summer Sports

Beautiful summer days, with their extra hours of daylight, are perfect for many different outdoor sports—whether you are competing yourself, just joining in for fun, or supporting your favorite team.

Venus Williams (above) started playing tennis when she was four years old. She has now won two of the four top Grand Slam titles in the world—Wimbledon (U.K.) in 2000 and 2001 and the U.S. Open in 2000. The other two main tournaments are held in France and Australia.

Cricket was first played in England over 300 years ago. The rules, decided in 1788, have survived almost unchanged to this day. Shaun Pollock (above), the captain of the South African cricket team, is considered one of the finest all-round players today.

Baseball is a direct descendant of two British games—cricket and rounders. Although baseball is played in over 120 countries around the world, including Japan and Australia, it is often known as the "national pastime" of the U.S. The major league baseball season lasts from early April until the World Series in October.

The first official baseball game was played between the Knickerbockers and the New York Nine in Hoboken, New Jersey, on October 21, 1845. Twenty three years later it became a professional game. Nowadays, there are 30 major league baseball teams throughout the United States and Canada, divided into the National League and the American League. Each season since 1903 the champions from each league have met in the World Series. Baseball was played for the first time as an official Olympic sport in Barcelona in 1992. At the Sydney Olympics in 2001, when professional athletes were allowed to compete, the United States defeated Cuba to win the gold medal.

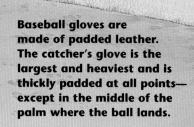

Baseball gloves are
made of padded leather.
The catcher's glove is the
largest and heaviest and is
thickly padded at all points—
except in the middle of the
palm where the ball lands.

Midnight sun festival

The summer solstice is the longest day and shortest night of the year. This is usually celebrated on December 21 or 22 in the Southern Hemisphere and June 21 or 22 in the Northern Hemisphere. In countries that lie to the extreme north, such as Alaska, Finland, and northern Sweden, the sun hardly ever sets at this time of year.

Midnight sun festivals are held in different parts of Alaska during the third week of June, with midnight baseball games, soccer tournaments, and marathon races that need no artificial lighting. The celebrations in the town of Nome take place in the far northwest of the country, just 100 mi. (164km) south of the Arctic Circle. At this time of year there are 22 hours of direct sunlight on the longest day, and the sun just touches the horizon at night but does not set. The midsummer events at Nome include a festival parade and the Nome river raft race (right).

O Bon is a Japanese festival that is usually held in mid-July or August for one week. It is the time when the souls of departed ancestors are believed to return home, and it has many different names, including "Feast of the Dead." Families clean their ancestors' graves and altars in their homes and decorate them with flowers. They also leave vegetables, fruit, and rice wine for the spirits to enjoy. Bright-red lanterns are hung up during the week to guide the spirits on their return. There are all kinds of different festivities, including fireworks at night.

Traditionally, midsummer has also been a time of celebration and festivities in northern European countries as the sun reaches its height in the sky. Over the centuries there have been many customs associated with it, mostly to do with lighting huge bonfires—perhaps to represent the sun—and dancing around them or even leaping through them!

Verona opera festival

Two thousand years ago the crowds in the Roman amphitheater in Verona, Italy, roared for their favorite gladiator as he fought for his life. Today the audiences in the amphitheater enjoy the music at the opera festival every summer.

Every year more than 500,000 visitors come to the historic town of Verona for the summer opera festival. It takes place every night of the season under the stars in the huge amphitheater, which can hold up to 15,000 spectators at a time.

The amphitheater was built between A.D. 0–100 during the last years of the Emperor Augustus, and it originally held 30,000 spectators. At the time it was the third-largest amphitheater in the world. It is remarkably well preserved, but it lost most of its outer ring in an earthquake that devastated the town in 1117. Over the years it has been the setting for a variety of spectacular events, including bloodthirsty gladiator contests, which were very popular in Roman times, as well as jousts and tournaments. It has been the home of the opera festival since 1913, but it is also a venue for ballets, jazz, and rock concerts.

Each night of the opera festival members of the audience can buy a little candle when they enter the amphitheater. As the opera begins the lights twinkle in the dusk.

In Kandy, Sri Lanka, the summer festival of Esala Perahera is held in honor of a single tooth, which is believed to have belonged to the Buddha. It is known as the "Relic" and is kept in a golden casket in the Dalada Maligawa—the Temple of the Tooth. On the final night of the festival a replica of the Relic is paraded through the streets under a canopy of lights. It is carried on an elephant known as the Maligawa Tusker.

FALL

Fall marks the turning of the year as the heat of summer fades. The harvest is brought in from the fields, and fruit is picked from the orchards. Animals are busy collecting food and storing it for the months ahead. The leaves on the trees start to change color and drop off the branches, swirling in the air in the blustery winds.

Fall winds

Fall is famous for its blustery weather and strong winds. They blow the leaves from the trees and make the clouds race across the sky. Since ancient times people have harnessed the wind's energy.

Wind is nothing more than moving air caused by the uneven heating of earth's surface by the sun and the different low and high air pressures around the world. Because earth spins on its axis, the air moves across the globe—in fact it flows in a curve. This is called the Coriolis effect. Air moving from the poles to the equator curves to the west. Air moving from the equator to the poles curves to the east.

More than 5,000 years ago the Egyptians used the wind to sail their ships on the Nile River. The Persians used windmills to grind their wheat and other grains. Today more and more electricity is being generated on wind farms. Wind machines are sometimes as tall as 10-story buildings. They have huge rotating blades that look like giant propellers—up to 60 ft. (18.3m) wide. The machines have to be as tall and wide as possible to catch more wind.

There are two different kinds of wind machines: one with a horizontal axis and the other with a vertical axis. They can operate only when the wind is blowing over 14 mph (22.5km/h), which occurs about 25 percent of the time. But when the wind is blowing harder than this, extra electricity is produced and stored in special batteries.

Wind is a clean, renewable energy source. It does not use up precious natural resources and will not run out, not as long as the sun keeps shining!

It is often very important to know what the wind conditions are, especially if you are going to sail a boat or fly a plane. The direction the wind is blowing from is displayed by a weather vane. This usually looks like an arrow with letters showing wind direction—for example, "E" for east. But the speed of the wind is measured by an anemometer that spins around in circles. The most common type looks like a small windmill with four cups attached to the central shaft (left). Wind speed is measured in knots for ships and aircraft, with one knot equal to 1.15 mph (1.85km/h). The Beaufort Scale, invented in 1805, measures wind speed as a "force" from 0 (calm, 0–0.6 mph/0–1km/h) to 12 (hurricane, over 74 mph/119km/h).

Fall colors

As the summer heat disappears nature struggles against the chills of the fall, putting on a spectacular display of color. Some trees turn coppery reds, bright oranges, and deep yellows, while nuts, berries, and toadstools burst into life, and flowers such as the purple crocus bloom.

Trees that lose their leaves are deciduous. Their leaves contain a special bright-green chemical called chlorophyll, which needs sunlight to produce food for the trees from air and water. As the sun's warmth fades during the fall leaves lose their shade of green and drop to the ground, and trees start to shut down for the winter.

The red maple is a stunning sight in the fall. Its leaves turn shades of orange or deep red as the shorter days cause chemical changes in the trees. Maples that turn red are usually male—female maples tend to be yellowy orange in color. Soil conditions also affect the color of the leaves—the more acid in the soil, the deeper the red.

As a species, the ginkgo biloba tree has been around for nearly 300 million years. Its distinctive, fan-shaped leaves turn yellow in the fall. Chemicals from its leaves and seeds are used to treat conditions such as memory loss and vertigo.

Aseroe rubra, which means "disgusting red," is a strange Australian fungus that grows in the fall. Also called the starfish stinkhorn, it oozes a strong-smelling slime that attracts flies. The flies spread the fungus' spores so that it can reproduce.

Coniferous trees, such as pines and firs, do not lose their leaves in the fall. Pine trees drop scaly cones. The scales open, releasing seeds in warm, dry weather and close in the cool and wet—so the cones can be used to forecast weather.

Fall fauna

In the fall animals and birds begin to get ready for the winter ahead. They stock up on food while there is plenty around and build cozy nests and shelters to keep themselves safe and warm.

Gray squirrels enjoy all kinds of different foods, depending on the season, and in the fall their diet usually consists of nuts, seeds, acorns, and berries.

Like many creatures, they eat as much as possible at this time of year so that they put on weight (layers of fat) to help them survive the winter. They collect extra food and bury it underground for later when it is scarce. They find these secret storages again months later by using their highly developed sense of smell. Occasionally a squirrel may forget about some food it buried, and the nuts will germinate and sprout into a clump of new trees. Squirrels sometimes make their homes in holes or cavities in tree trunks. But they often build large nests made out of leaves and twigs near the tops of large trees. These are known as drays and can be seen in the bare branches as the winter approaches.

Many creatures that hibernate prepare their winter homes during the fall months. Hedgehogs make their large nests in sheltered spots where they can curl up tight for four or five months. It might be under a pile of leaves or an old compost heap or in the root of a tree.

Every fall millions of monarch butterflies gather in southern Canada and then migrate thousands of miles south to Central America.

The fox has a tawny coat and white-tipped brush, or tail. As the winter approaches the fur becomes thicker to keep out the bitter cold.

Jays pick acorns from oak trees. They fly off with them in their beaks and bury them in the ground. In the winter they return to their food hiding spots.

Badgers prepare their setts by lining them with moist leaves that generate warmth and by blocking passages to keep out the cold and intruders.

63

Fall farming

Fall is harvesttime in most countries; farms are at their busiest and many major crops are ready to be brought in. Farmers look to the skies and hope for good weather in the coming weeks.

After long days of summer sun the fields of corn, wheat, oats, and barley are ripe. Giant machines called combines work night and day, cutting the crops and bringing in the harvest before the weather breaks.

The trees in the apple orchard are heavy with fruit, which is picked by hand as quickly as possible before it becomes too ripe. The apples bruise very easily, even though their flesh is firm, so they have to be handled gently. Each one is carefully placed in a basket before being transferred into large, wooden crates. The apples are washed, sorted, and packed, and then some are sent off to be sold while others are kept in cool storage areas until later in the year—or used to make cider or apple juice. There are thousands of different varieties of apples, each with its own special flavor and texture.

By the time the fall has arrived, vineyards are thick and green, and the vines are heavy with bunches of sweet, juicy grapes that are ready to be picked. As the grapes ripen, they are checked for acidity and sugar levels. In all the great wine regions of the world—including France, Australia, California, and South Africa—the harvest (or *vendange*) is the great event of the year. In many European vineyards grapes are still picked by hand, but machines are being used more and more.

64

Fall and us

Leaves have
usually turned
from green to brown
by the time they drop
off the trees. They have lost
all their moisture and are
dry and crunchy underfoot.

Fall is a time for raking up the leaves in the yard and lighting bonfires, for collecting chestnuts and picking mushrooms. Although the days are getting shorter, the weather can be beautiful before winter sets in.

When a bonfire has burned out, gardeners scatter the ashes that are left—which are full of nutrients—around their plants.

By mid-October the leaves have fallen everywhere, covering the grass and hiding footpaths, filling up drains and blocking gutters. In some places people rake them up and burn huge bonfires that slowly burn for days, the smoke spiraling into the air. In many places burning leaves is not allowed, so the raked leaves are placed in garbage bags and put out for collection.

Chestnuts are the seeds of the horse chestnut tree. They are eaten by deer, cattle, and in the past were sometimes ground up for sheep.

This is the chestnut season, when the prickly green cases that drop from horse chestnut trees open up to reveal glossy brown nuts inside. A popular children's game played in the U.K. is "conkers," where two players attempt to smash each other's horse chestnut or "conker" (the conker is threaded onto a piece of string) by taking turns swinging at it. Adults play as well; each year, the World Conker Championships are held in October in Northamptonshire in the U.K. Hundreds of contestants from all over the world take part.

Fungi, such as toadstools and mushrooms, appear in woods, meadows, and gardens. Some fungi are edible, but always check with an adult first.

There are many things to do in the yard at this time of year. Plants need to be cut back and cleaned up, and mulch can be made from leaves to use as fertilizer next year. Bulbs can be planted so that they will flower in the spring. Birds are preparing for the winter, so it is a good idea to put nuts and seeds out for them.

Native Americans preserved blackberries by drying them. The berries were then mixed with dried meat to make pemmican.

Up in the air

Fall days are perfect for flying kites. They soar through the air almost with a life of their own, dancing at the end of their long, thin lines.

The basic kite is a simple two-stick kite often known as a diamond. It has one line and usually has a very long tail.

Some kites are highly decorated and brightly colored. They look like beautiful birds or insects flying through the sky.

No one is exactly sure when kites were invented, but they have certainly been swooping through the skies in various forms for more than two thousand years. Over the centuries they have been used in various—and sometimes surprising—ways.

In New Zealand the Maori people made kites in the shapes of birds to carry messages to the gods. Stories from ancient China describe daring exploits in times of war, when soldiers were hoisted into the air on large kites to spy over enemy territories. Other tales tell of kites equipped with whistles that screamed through the night skies to terrify the opposing army. The Wright brothers used kites to test their theories for the first flying machine. More recently special kites have been used to carry meteorological instruments to learn more about the planet's weather.

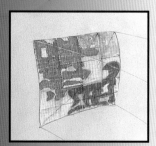

Stunt kites have two or more control lines with handles so that they can be steered through the sky to perform tricks.

The Japanese Sagami Giant kite is 155 sq. ft. (14.4 sq. m), weighs almost 1,940 lbs (880kg), and needs 90 people to hoist it up into the air.

Kites come in all kinds of different shapes and sizes and are made out of the latest, hi-tech materials, which are both tough and light. Diamond, delta, and dragon kites fly well in light to medium winds, while box kites fly better when the winds are much stronger.

Thanksgiving

Thanksgiving, on the fourth Thursday in November, is perhaps one of the greatest celebrations of the year in the United States. Families across the country sit down together to enjoy a traditional Thanksgiving feast.

The history of Thanksgiving dates back many centuries to the Pilgrims' very first harvest in 1621. They had endured terrible hardships during their first year in the New World. Secure in the knowledge that they now had enough food for the winter, they sat down with their native American neighbors, who taught them about how to grow crops such as corn, to give thanks.

Festivals of light, which mark the approach of winter, are found in many cultures around the world. The Hindu celebration of Diwali (Deepavali) lasts for five days and gets its name from the tiny clay lamps, known as *diyas*, that are lit in every home after sunset. There are many traditions to be observed, such as decorating the cattle or taking ritual baths.

In 1817 New York State adopted Thanksgiving Day as an annual custom, and by the mid-1800s many other states also celebrated a Thanksgiving Day. In 1863 President Abraham Lincoln appointed a national Day of Thanksgiving on the last Thursday in November, but this was changed by President Franklin Delano Roosevelt in 1939 to the fourth Thursday in November. However, in Canada, Thanksgiving is always celebrated on the second Monday in October.

Turkey, cranberry sauce, sweet potatoes, green beans, fresh bread, and pumpkin pie are usually served at a typical Thanksgiving meal. The Pilgrims, who had been shown how to catch wild turkeys and grow new crops by the native Americans, probably enjoyed a similar feast.

Chinese moon festival

The moon festival is celebrated by Chinese communities around the world on the 15th day of the eighth month of the Chinese year. Because this is lunar—governed by the moon—the exact date is not always the same, but it usually falls in September or October in the western calendar.

During the moon festival, people celebrate the harvest moon, which is at its brightest and fullest and hangs like an enormous disk in the fall sky. Traditionally they give thanks for the crops that they have gathered from the fields and are grateful that the hard work of harvesting is over for another year.

Families and friends enjoy a special feast and decorate their houses with bright lanterns, often shaped like animals. They admire the splendid moon—as long as it is a clear and cloudless night—and think about the moon goddess, Chang-O, who is said to have floated up to the moon long ago after drinking the elixir of everlasting life. Moon festival altars are laden with dishes of round fruits, such as apples, peaches, and small melons, to symbolize the moon as well as family togetherness. Special moon cakes are baked and eaten. They are piled up in little groups (pyramids) of 13 to represent the 13 lunar months in the Chinese calendar.

Halloween, celebrated on the night of October 31, used to be known as the "night of the dead." It was believed that ghosts returned to roam the earth—and witches and evil spirits were out in force on the eve of All Saints' Day on November 1. Traditionally people have always been up to mischief on Halloween—today children dress up in costumes and go out trick-or-treating for goodies as soon as it gets dark. Houses display carved jack-o'-lanterns to light their way. Children should always be accompanied by an adult when they go out trick-or-treating.

WINTER

Winter brings frost and snow, and temperatures can drop below the freezing point. The sun is pale and low in the sky now, and its rays have lost their strength. Some creatures curl up and go to sleep for the winter months, safe in their underground burrows. Others set off on their long migration to warmer places.

Winter chills

In the winter the sun hangs low in the sky, and its rays generate less warmth. As temperatures fall weather conditions can quickly change, with sleet, snow-, and hailstorms.

During the winter months the days are short and cold and the nights are long and dark. The winter solstice, on December 21 or 22 in the Northern Hemisphere and June 21 or 22 in the Southern Hemisphere, is the shortest day of the entire year.

The reindeer—or caribou—has a thick coat for warmth and splayed hooves for walking on snow.

Birds of prey—such as buzzards—are skillful hunters, but food is scarce when snow covers the ground.

When the temperature has dropped below the freezing point, dripping water forms icicles.

The tough, strong needles of pine and fir trees stand up to the harshest winters and the thickest snow.

Small birds—like the wren—are protected from the cold by their feathers, but they often go hungry.

High winds sometimes whip up blizzards when it is snowing heavily and cause deep snow drifts.

When it is very cold, tiny droplets of water inside clouds freeze and form minute ice crystals. The crystals join up with each other, making the most delicate and intricate patterns, and turn into snowflakes. Each snowflake has at least 50 individual ice crystals in it. And although every snowflake has six sides or six points, no two snowflakes are the same. The exact shape that the crystals make depends on the air temperature.

In the depths of winter, when the temperature drops below 32°F (0°C), ponds, lakes, streams, and rivers may freeze. But the sea does not start to ice over until it is much colder (28°F/–2°C) because of its very high salt content.

Hibernation

Some creatures, such as gray squirrels, shrews, and foxes, are active throughout the winter months—as long as they can find food. Others, including bears, bats, chipmunks, snakes, and mosquitoes, survive the winter by hibernating.

Hibernation is a very deep sleep that can last for days, weeks, or months. It is a way of getting through the winter when food is scarce.

True hibernation can last for months. It is a state of complete inactivity when the body temperature drops to around 40°F (5°C), and the heartbeat and breathing slow down dramatically. Very little energy is used. During the fall the creature will have prepared for hibernation by eating extra food and storing it up as body fat to use for energy during the long winter ahead.

Ground squirrels and bats are true hibernators and sleep so deeply that they are almost impossible to wake up. But from time to time their body temperatures return to normal, and they wake up. They are then active for a day or so before returning to their deep sleep again. When they are asleep, they are completely defenseless, so it is important that they find somewhere secure to make their winter homes—hidden away from hungry predators.

Bears sleep between three to seven months a year, starting in the early winter. During this time they do not eat, drink, urinate, or defecate—thus they lose one quarter of their normal body weight.

The dormouse is known as the "sleeping mouse" from the French word *dormir*, which means "to sleep." It can spend up to eight months each year hibernating in its shallow underground nest.

Chipmunks stock their burrows with large amounts of seeds to see them through the winter. They wake up from time to time, have a bite to eat, and then go back to sleep for a while.

78

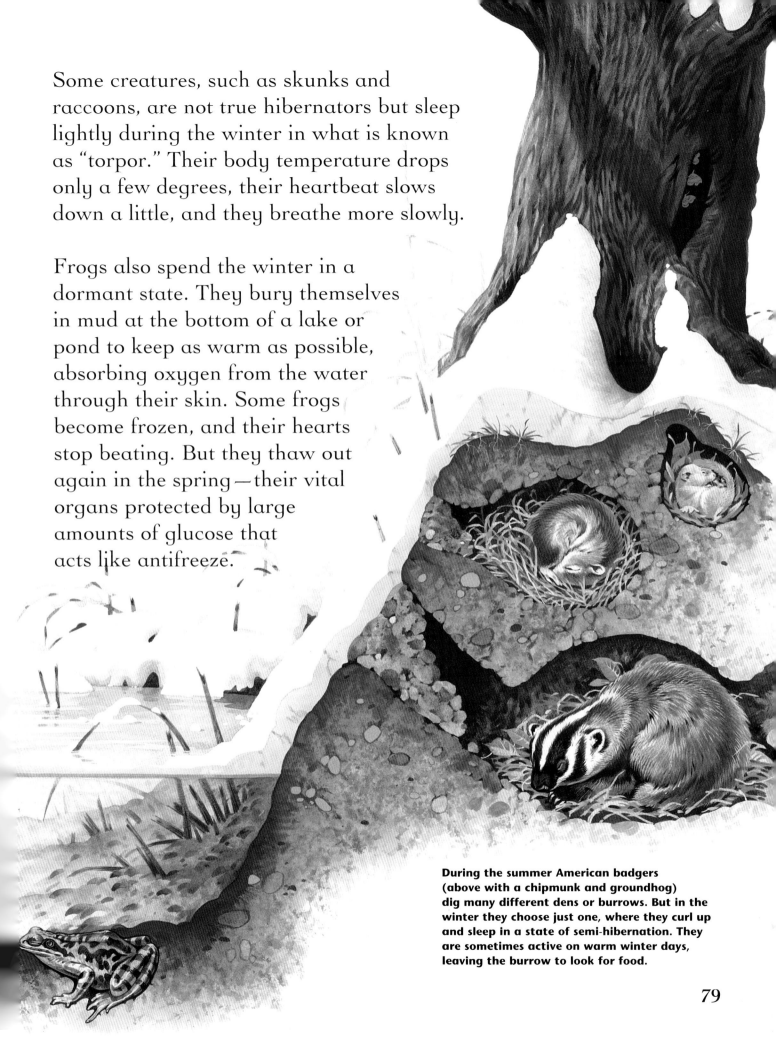

Some creatures, such as skunks and raccoons, are not true hibernators but sleep lightly during the winter in what is known as "torpor." Their body temperature drops only a few degrees, their heartbeat slows down a little, and they breathe more slowly.

Frogs also spend the winter in a dormant state. They bury themselves in mud at the bottom of a lake or pond to keep as warm as possible, absorbing oxygen from the water through their skin. Some frogs become frozen, and their hearts stop beating. But they thaw out again in the spring—their vital organs protected by large amounts of glucose that acts like antifreeze.

During the summer American badgers (above with a chipmunk and groundhog) dig many different dens or burrows. But in the winter they choose just one, where they curl up and sleep in a state of semi-hibernation. They are sometimes active on warm winter days, leaving the burrow to look for food.

Migration

Many animals, birds, and fish migrate with the changing seasons. As the winter approaches some leave the cold regions, where they breed in the summer, and set off on their long journey in search of warmth, shelter, and food.

Every year creatures of all shapes and sizes — including whales, butterflies, geese, caribou, and wildebeest — make the journey between their summer and winter homes. They use the same route year after year — and generation after generation.

Some migrating animals do not travel far, perhaps just a few hundred miles, but others cover incredible distances. The current record is held by the Arctic tern, which travels over 10,000 mi. (16,000km) from the North Pole to the South Pole and back again every year.

Birds usually migrate in large flocks. They use the stars and the sun to help them navigate—as well as major landmarks on the ground like coastlines, rivers, and mountain ranges. Some people think that they also use earth's magnetic field to help them find their way. In the United States migration is usually in a north-south direction along four major routes known as "flyways." In Europe these migration routes follow a more east-west direction. But wherever they are flying, migrating birds need the wind behind them, clear days, and starry skies for a good flight.

On the vast plains of East Africa huge herds of wildebeest—or gnus—migrate nearly 1,865 mi. (3,000km) each year in search of grass and water. They have to drink every two days, and so they have to live near a source of water. In the rainy season over 1.4 million wildebeest arrive in the grasslands of the southern Serengeti, where there is plenty of food and water.

Long, straggling lines— or skeins—of Brant geese fly high in the sky as they leave the Arctic and head south to the shores of the Atlantic and Pacific oceans, where they will live on eelgrass all winter long. They fly fast, taking occasional breaks.

Wintertime

When winter arrives and the weather gets cold, it is vital to keep warm. If your temperature drops just a few degrees too low, it can be a matter of life and death.

The human body has evolved many ways to try and keep warm, such as shivering. When you shiver, your muscles automatically tighten up and relax very quickly, burning more food for energy and creating warmth. Your teeth often chatter at the same time, having the same result. Goose bumps appear when tiny muscles pull the thin hairs on the skin up straight in an attempt to trap warm air.

Over the centuries we have devised all kinds of things to keep out the chills on a cold winter's night. A heated brick or a heavy stone bottle (right) filled with hot water were often used to warm the sheets before rubber hot-water bottles and electric blankets came along. A big, brass warming pan, full of red-hot coals, was another solution. It had a long, wooden handle and a lid with little holes on it to let the smoke out.

New outdoor clothing, made of the latest hi-tech materials, keep you warm even when it is freezing cold. But now new battery-heated clothing is being developed for people who have to go out in bitterly cold weather—such as rescue teams or mountain climbers. The fabric has heat-conducting metal filaments woven into it, which are connected to a small, portable battery.

Winter farming

Winter is one of the quietest times of the year on the farm, when you cannot see very much happening. But it is just as important as any other season in the farming year.

In the winter, as temperatures drop, thick frosts freeze the soil in the bare fields and help break it up. Snow and ice accumulate deep in the ground and then melt in the spring and water the new crops. A new layer of rich topsoil slowly forms, made of dead plants and organic debris. In warmer weather this topsoil would be devoured by insects, but in the winter they are fast asleep (hibernating) to avoid the cold.

Fresh grass is scarce, so cattle are brought in to barns and sheds where they can be fed and kept warm and dry. Sheep, which are more hardy, often stay out all winter. If the ground is covered with snow, the farmer will take bales of hay to them in the pastures.

Pineapples are grown in tropical and semitropical countries where it is hot all the time—they do not have a winter season. The main producers are Hawaii and Malaysia. Because there is no winter, they can grow and harvest pineapples all year round. The plants are grown from the spiky crowns (or tops) of other pineapples that are planted in the fields—it takes about 18 months to produce the first fruits. Planting takes place through the year to make sure that there is always a good supply of pineapples, ready to be shipped off all over the world. They are picked when they are ready to eat. Like strawberries, they do not continue to ripen after they have been picked.

Winter playtime

When a blanket of fresh, white snow covers the ground, the world is transformed. It does not matter where you live—in the city or in the country—everything looks brand new. Everyone wants to go outside to ice-skate, sled, or build huge snowmen.

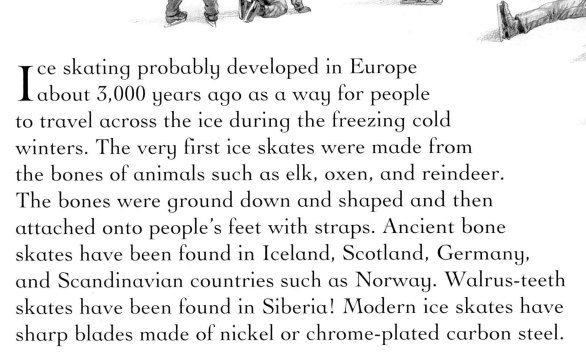

Ice skating probably developed in Europe about 3,000 years ago as a way for people to travel across the ice during the freezing cold winters. The very first ice skates were made from the bones of animals such as elk, oxen, and reindeer. The bones were ground down and shaped and then attached onto people's feet with straps. Ancient bone skates have been found in Iceland, Scotland, Germany, and Scandinavian countries such as Norway. Walrus-teeth skates have been found in Siberia! Modern ice skates have sharp blades made of nickel or chrome-plated carbon steel.

Today most people ice-skate for fun—not out of necessity. In 1876 the world's first refrigerated ice-skating rink, the Glaciarium, was opened in London, England. Then three years later the first indoor rink opened in New York City. Indoor ice-skating rinks are cooled by the same technology that works in refrigerators. The surface of the ice is kept smooth and clean by ice-resurfacing machines.

Sleds come in all shapes and sizes and can be made of wood, metal, or plastic. The fronts are often bent up and over to form hoods. Ropes are attached so that passengers can hold on.

The traditional snowman has a bright-orange carrot for a nose and two black eyes made out of pieces of coal. Ice and snow can also be used to make more complicated sculptures, like the ones made every January at The St. Paul Winter Carnival in Minnesota.

WARNING: Only skate at ice rinks when you are accompanied by an adult. Never skate on frozen lakes, ponds, or rivers—ice breaks easily. Always ask an adult for permission before you go out sledding or playing in the snow.

Winter Sports

Skiing is one of the most thrilling winter sports—whether you are a beginner or an expert racing down the mountain at almost 60 mph (100km/h).

Winter mountaineering can be difficult and dangerous. It is the most challenging time of year, with freezing temperatures and biting winds. Serious climbers are extremely athletic and take no risks, following very specific procedures as they trek across snow, rock, and ice. They wear layers of protective clothing to keep warm—hats or balaclavas, gloves, goggles, and crampons on their boots. They carry ice picks and ropes as well. If they get into difficulty, mountain rescue teams are always on call.

Downhill skiing first started in the Alps in Europe and is often known as Alpine skiing. There are thousands of ski areas in the world—most of them in Europe, Canada, the United States, and Japan.

World Cup ski competitions are held every year in Northern Hemisphere countries from December to March.

The World Ski Championships are held every other year, and the Winter Olympics take place every four years. There are five different kinds of races in Alpine competitions: the downhill, the slalom, the giant slalom, the super giant slalom, and the parallel slalom. In slalom races the competitors have to ski between a series of "gates" made out of pairs of poles laid out in a zigzag pattern down the course.

Snowboarding evolved from skiing, skateboarding, and surfing. It began in the United States in the 1960s.

Ski poles are made of aluminum or composite materials. They have a round or star-shaped piece of plastic called a basket, about 3 in. (8cm) from the bottom—this prevents the pole from sinking into the snow. Ski boots consist of an outer shell made from hard plastic and an inner boot made out of foam.

Sapporo's snow festival

Japan's biggest snow festival is held in February in Sapporo on the island of Hokkaido. The festival, known as Yuki Matsuri in Japan, began in 1950 and now attracts around two million people each year.

Huge sculptures of famous buildings and monuments, fantastic creatures, and cartoon characters are carved out of snow and ice—all in incredible detail. Life-size, multistory ice buildings are illuminated and are even big enough for visitors to wander around inside. Some are almost 50 ft. (15m) high. Over the years snow and ice replicas of many of the world's most famous landmarks have been made, including the Egyptian pyramids, St. Paul's Cathedral in London, the Taj Mahal in India, and the Great Wall of China. Over 3,000 sculptors take part—spending almost one month carving out the huge constructions and often working at night. Trucks carry fresh loads of clean snow down from the mountains, and bulldozers push the snow into position.

Makara Sakranti is the winter solstice in the Hindu calendar and is marked by the passing of the sun into the sign (*Sakranti*) of Capricorn (*Makara*). It takes place in the middle of the winter—usually around January 14 or 15—and there are many festivals all over India to celebrate the harvest and the coming of spring. In the south the festival is known as Pongal. It gets its name from a special rice dish that is offered to the rain and sun gods. Pongal is also offered to the cattle, honoring them for their hard work.

In 1972 the snow festival was
held during the eleventh Winter
Olympic Games in Sapporo, which
gave it tremendous publicity around
the world. As a result the International Snow Statue
Competition began in 1974, and now teams from all over
the world take part. They include groups from Hawaii and
Southeast Asian countries where it never snows, and their
only experience of ice sculpting is on a much smaller scale.

New Year's

On New Year's Eve (December 31 in many countries) people all over the world stay up until midnight to celebrate the New Year.

At the stroke of midnight a huge fireworks display starts on the battlements of Edinburgh Castle in Scotland, perched high up on the hill.

In Scotland, New Year's is known as Hogmanay, the most important festival of the year—it draws huge crowds in cities such as Edinburgh and Glasgow. Although New Year's is celebrated far and wide, some communities (for example Hindus, Muslims, and the Chinese) use different calendars, and so it falls at another time of the year.

There are different opinions about where the word "Hogmanay" came from—possibly the Gaelic *oge maidne* which means "new morning."

But everybody agrees that the roots of Hogmanay reach back to the time when primitive people worshiped sun and fire in the deep winter. Over the years this changed and developed into the great Roman winter festival of Saturnalia, a time of riotous festivities.

Today there are enormous gatherings in downtown areas of large cities like New York, Sydney, and London. At the stroke of midnight in Times Square in New York City, a huge ball covered in lightbulbs is lowered down, glittering with its lights. In Sydney, Australia, a spectacular fireworks display takes place in the harbor. In London, England, crowds sing "Auld Lang Syne" in the famous Trafalgar Square.

Hogmanay traditions include "first footing." On the last stroke of midnight a dark-haired man is invited into the house. He must bring some coal (for warmth), bread (for food), and a coin (for wealth).

Groundhog Day, on February 2 every year, is now an important event in the United States. The Mayor and citizens of Punxsutawney, Pennsylvania, gather to watch a groundhog named Phil emerge from his winter sleep. If it is sunny and Phil sees his own shadow, he has another six weeks' nap, but if it is cloudy he stays out, and the prediction is for fair weather.

SEASONAL EVENTS

JANUARY
NEW YEAR'S DAY
MAKARA SAKRANTI (HINDU)
MARTIN LUTHER KING, JR.'S
BIRTHDAY

FEBRUARY
CHINESE NEW YEAR
SAPPORO'S SNOW FESTIVAL
ASH WEDNESDAY (CHRISTIAN)
VALENTINE'S DAY
PRESIDENT'S DAY

MARCH
AL HIJRAH (MUSLIM NEW YEAR)
ST. PATRICK'S DAY (CHRISTIAN)
VERNAL EQUINOX:
SPRING BEGINS
PASSOVER; (JEWISH)
GOOD FRIDAY (CHRISTIAN)

APRIL
DAYLIGHT SAVING TIME BEGINS
EASTER (CHRISTIAN)

MAY
CINCO DE MAYO (MEXICAN
INDEPENDENCE DAY)
MOTHER'S DAY
BUN BANG FAI
MEMORIAL DAY

JUNE
SUMMER SOLSTICE:
SUMMER BEGINS
FLAG DAY
FATHER'S DAY

JULY
FOURTH OF JULY
(U.S. INDEPENDENCE DAY)

SEPTEMBER
LABOR DAY
ROSH HASHANAH
(JEWISH NEW YEAR)
YOM KIPPUR (DAY OF
ATONEMENT; JEWISH)
FALL EQUINOX:
FALL BEGINS

OCTOBER
NAVARATRI
(1ST DAY; HINDU)
DAYLIGHT SAVING TIME ENDS
UNITED NATIONS DAY
HALLOWEEN

NOVEMBER
ALL SAINTS' DAY (CHRISTIAN)
DIWALI (1ST DAY; HINDU)
RAMADAN (1ST DAY; MUSLIM)
ELECTION DAY
VETERANS DAY
THANKSGIVING

DECEMBER
CHANUKKAH (JEWISH)
ID AL-FITR (END OF
RAMADAN; MUSLIM)
WINTER SOLSTICE:
WINTER BEGINS
CHRISTMAS DAY (CHRISTIAN)
NEW YEAR'S EVE

INDEX

Alaska 52
ancient Egyptians 45, 59
ancient Romans 55
animals 10, 13, 22–23, 40–41,
   62–63, 77, 78–79, 80–81
Antarctica 10
apples 64

baseball 50–51
beach vacations 48–49
birds 23, 28, 63, 67, 77, 80–81
bonfires 33, 53, 67
Buddhism 55
Bun Bang Fai 34–35

camels 10, 41
chestnuts 67
China 68, 72–73
clothes 19, 27, 83, 88
clouds 14, 19
cold 10, 76–77, 82–83
constellations 30–31

deserts 10
Diwali (Deepavali) 70, 95
dogs 28, 29, 41

electricity 45, 59
elephants 40–41, 55
Esala Perahera 55

fall 8, 9, 56–72
farming 24, 46, 64, 84
festivals 32–35, 46, 52–55,
   70–73, 90–95
flowers 18, 20–21, 22, 46, 47
frogs 23, 79
fruit 46, 64, 67, 72, 84
fungi 60, 67

global warming 9, 38
gods and goddesses 27, 34,
   45, 72
Groundhog Day 93

Halloween 72
harvest 64, 72
heat 10, 12–13, 39, 40–41,
   44–45
hibernation 63, 78–79, 84
Hinduism 33, 70, 90
Hogmanay 92–93
Holi 33
Holland 20
honeybees 42–43
human body 45, 83
hurricanes 15

ice 10, 45, 77, 84
ice sculpting 90–91
ice-skating 86–87
insects 20, 22, 42, 63, 84
Inuit 34
Ireland 32–33
Italy 54–55

Japan 52, 68, 90–91

Kalahari bushmen 12
keeping cool 40–41, 45
kites 68–69

lambs 24–25
leaves 60–61, 66–67

Maori people 68
Mars 9, 30
meteor showers 31
midnight sun 52–53
migration 63, 80–81
moon festival 72–73

native Americans 46, 67

New Year's 92–93
night 30–31, 52–53, 76, 83

O Bon 52
opera festival 54–55

parks 28–29
penguins 10–11
planets 9, 30
pond life 22–23

rain 18–19, 34
rainbows 19
rocket festival 34–35

St. Patrick's Day 32–33
savannas 12–13
Scotland 92–93
seasons, cause of 9, 38–39
skateboarding 28
skiing 88–89
snow 76–77, 84–87
snow festival 90–91
solstices 38–39, 52, 76, 90
sports 50–51, 88–89
spring 8, 9, 16–33
spring cleaning 26–27
spring equinox 27
Sri Lanka 55
summer 8, 9, 36–55
sun 9, 12, 18, 38–39, 44–45,
   52–53, 60, 76
sunflowers 46–47

Thailand 34–35
Thanksgiving 70–71
Toonik Tyme 34
tornados 14
trees 12, 18, 20, 28, 29,
   60–61, 77

U.S. 33, 50, 70–71, 87, 93

water 10, 12–13, 40, 41, 84
weather 6, 18–19, 68
winds 14–15, 58–59, 77
winter 9, 74–93